J 973.04966
Keedl
Keedle, Jayne

West African Americans

West African Americans

by Jayne Keedle

Series Consultant: Judith A. Warner, Ph.D.,
Professor of Sociology and Criminal Justice,
Texas A&M International University

Marshall Cavendish
Benchmark
New York

Marshall Cavendish Benchmark
99 White Plains Road
Tarrytown, NY 10591
www.marshallcavendish.us

Library of Congress Cataloging-in-Publication Data

Keedle, Jayne.
    West African Americans / by Jayne Keedle.
        p. cm. — (New Americans)
    Includes bibliographical references and index.
    ISBN 978-0-7614-4313-1
    1. West Africans—United States—Juvenile literature. 2. African
Americans—United States—Juvenile literature. 3. Africa, West—Emigration
and immigration—History—Juvenile literature. 4. United States—Emigration
and immigration—History—Juvenile literature. I. Title.
    E184.A24K44 2010
    973'.04966--dc22   2008055753

Developed for Marshall Cavendish Benchmark by RJF Publishing LLC
Robert Famighetti, President
www.RJFpublishing.com
Design: Westgraphix LLC/Tammy West
Photo Research: Edward A. Thomas
Map Illustrator: Stefan Chabluk
Index: Nila Glikin

CONTENTS

Words defined in the glossary are in **bold** type
the first time they appear in the text.

INTRODUCTION

The United States has embraced immigration for most of its history—and has been a destination of choice for people seeking a better life. Today hundreds of thousands of immigrants arrive each year to live and work and make their way in a new country. These "New Americans" come for many reasons, and they come from places all over the world. They bring with them new customs, languages, and traditions—and face many challenges in their adopted country. Over time, they and their children are changed by and become part of the American mainstream culture. At the same time, the mainstream is itself changed as it absorbs many elements of the immigrants' cultures, from ethnic foods to ideas from non-Western belief systems. An understanding of the New Americans, and how they will form part of the American future, is essential for everyone.

This series focuses on recent immigrants from eight major countries and regions: the Caribbean and Central America, China, India and other South Asian countries, Korea, Mexico, Russia and Eastern Europe, Southeast Asia, and West Africa.

Each of these geographic areas is a major source of the millions of immigrants who have come to the United States in the last decades of the twentieth century and the beginning of the twenty-first. For many of these people, the opportunity to move to the United States was opened up by the major

New Americans being sworn in as U.S. citizens.

changes in U.S. immigration law that occurred in the 1960s. For others, the opportunity or imperative to immigrate was triggered by events in their own countries, such as the collapse of Communism in Eastern Europe or civil wars in Central America.

Some of the New Americans found sizable communities of Americans from the same ethnic background and had the benefit of "ethnic neighborhoods" to move into where they could feel welcome and get help adjusting to American life. Many of these communities originated in a previous major wave of immigration, from the 1880s to 1920. Some of the New Americans found very few predecessors to ease the transition as they faced the challenges of adjustment.

These volumes tell the stories of the New Americans, including the personal accounts of a number of immigrants and their children who agreed to be interviewed by some of the authors. As you read, you will learn about the countries of origin and the cultures of these newcomers to American society. You will learn, as well, about how the New Americans are enriching, as they adapt to, American life.

Judith A. Warner, Ph.D.
Professor of Sociology and Criminal Justice
Texas A&M International University

The owner/chef of a West African restaurant outside Washington, D.C., puts the finishing touches on one of his creations.

CHAPTER ONE

THE WEST AFRICAN-AMERICAN COMMUNITY TODAY

The smell of African-made incense sweetens the air at the Clark Park People's Flea Market in Southwest Philadelphia. From spring to fall, street vendors set up shop at the outdoor market. Their wares range from traditional African carvings and woven straw baskets to baseball caps and books. Stalls selling CDs pound out infectious beats by traditional West African drummers and modern-day hip hop artists. The market raises money for the Uhuru Movement, a group that supports political and charitable causes in West Africa. Immigrants from the region keep close ties to their home countries.

Thousands of African immigrants have settled in the Philadelphia area. Most of them come from the West African countries of Liberia, Sierra Leone, Ghana, Nigeria, Côte d'Ivoire (Ivory Coast), and Senegal. Each country has its own unique cultures, traditions, languages, and religions. In Nigeria alone, there are 250 different ethnic groups. At West African restaurants and hair-braiding salons along Philadelphia's Woodland Avenue, conversations flow freely in many languages, including the West African languages of Yoruba, Hausa, and Ibo. West African restaurants offer immigrants a taste of home cooking, serving spicy peanut and mutton stews and rice dishes. There are no mashed potatoes on the menus here. Instead, there is fufu, which is a porridge-like mash that can be made from a wide variety of vegetables or fruits, including yams, corn, and bananas. Forks are for the American-born. The newest West-African arrivals use their fingers to form the fufu into balls that they dip into spicy sauces.

Philadelphia has been an important center for African-American culture and history for centuries. It was here that the **abolitionist** movement against slavery grew strong. In the eighteenth century, Philadelphia had the largest population of free blacks in the United States. Today, the city still is home to many African Americans. Since the 1990s, the black population has swelled with a growing number of immigrants from West Africa.

By the Numbers

At the beginning of the twenty-first century, Philadelphia was among the U.S. metropolitan areas with the largest African-born populations. Others included Washington, D.C., New York City, Atlanta, Minneapolis-Saint Paul, Boston, Los Angeles, Houston, Chicago, and Dallas. The West

States with the Most Nigerian Americans

Texas	24,204
New York	21,945
Maryland	17,700
California	16,198
Georgia	10,989
New Jersey	9,551
Illinois	8,842
Florida	5,219
Massachusetts	4,056
North Carolina	3,858

Source: U.S. Bureau of the Census, 2000 Census data.
Note: Census Bureau 2006 population estimates do not give breadowns by state for states with fewer than 65,000 Nigerian Americans.

African–born population of Detroit was growing rapidly in the early years of the twenty-first century. According to Census data, New York's African immigrant population more than doubled between 1990 and 2000, to nearly 74,000 people. The Washington, D.C., area had the largest concentration of African-born immigrants in 2000—more than 80,000 people.

While some immigrant groups are concentrated in just a handful of states, West Africans are more widely scattered across the United States. About 15 percent live in rural areas and small towns in states such as North Dakota, Nebraska, Maine, Ohio, Michigan, and Washington. About 20 percent reside in Midwestern states, and 15 percent live in Western states.

People of Nigerian birth—numbering more than 155,000 people in 2006—represent the largest group of immigrants from West Africa. The next largest groups come from Ghana, Liberia, Cameroon, Cape Verde (an island nation about 350 miles [560 kilometers] west of the African coast), Sierra Leone, Côte d'Ivoire, and Senegal.

West Africans are among the smaller immigrant groups in the United States, but their numbers are increasing. According to U.S. Census Bureau estimates, about 490,000 people of West African descent were living in the United States in 2006. That figure represented an increase of more than 16,000 people since 2005. People of Nigerian descent made up the largest portion of the 2006 population. According to Census estimates, there were almost 238,000 Nigerian Americans living in the United States

A shop in Philadelphia offers West African-style hair braiding. Philadelphia is one of the American cities with a large African-born population.

in 2006. Census data also indicate that more than half of all African immigrants are recent arrivals, having entered the United States since 1990.

The People

Many West Africans came to the United States in the 1960s and 1970s, when a number of West African countries gained their independence from Great Britain, France, and other European colonial rulers. Many of these arrivals came as students to attend American universities. After graduation, most returned to help their newly independent nations develop, but some stayed.

By the 1980s, however, more people from West Africa were coming to the United States to stay, and that trend has continued. Many young African nations have struggled with political unrest, corruption, and high rates of poverty and unemployment. Some have been torn apart by civil wars. The result has been two major types of immigrants.

One type consists of people who are better off economically, who tend to be better educated and to have strong job skills, and who have come to the United States looking for greater safety, stability, and opportunity. These immigrants include many highly educated professionals, such as doctors, teachers, nurses, engineers, and lawyers. Those who come from former British colonies, such as Nigeria and Ghana, speak English well. That makes it easier for them to find jobs and adjust to life in the United States. Among Nigerian-American adults living in the United States in 2006, almost two-thirds had at least a bachelor's degree, compared to less than one-third of adults in the U.S. population as a whole.

Another type of West-African immigrant consists of **refugees** needing a safe haven. These are people who have been forced to flee their homes and often their home countries. They may have been under attack because of their political or religious beliefs, or because they belong to a particular ethnic group, or even just because they were caught in the middle of the fighting. In recent years, civil wars in West African countries have produced an increasing number of refugees. These immigrants are not as likely to be well-educated as other West African immigrants, and they have more difficulty finding employment and otherwise settling in.

Not all West African immigrants fall into these two categories, of course. No matter what prompts them to leave their home country, relatively few of them are **undocumented** immigrants. Before they come to the

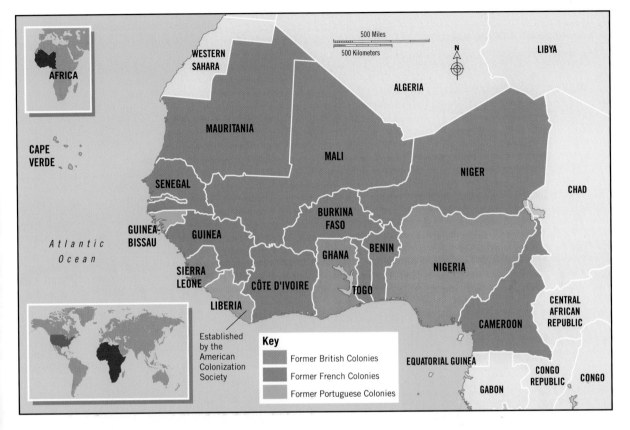

Most West African countries are former colonies of Great Britain, France, or Portugal. Many gained their independence in the 1960s and 1970s.

United States, most obtain **visas** from the U.S. government allowing them to live and work permanently in the United States.

The most common type of undocumented immigrants from West Africa are people who enter the United States with student, tourist, or other visas allowing them to stay in the country for only a limited period of time. Some of these people simply stay in the United States without authorization after their temporary visas have expired.

From the 1600s to the 1800s, half a million West Africans were brought to the United States as slaves. Shown here: slaves pick cotton on a plantation near Savannah, Georgia.

CHAPTER TWO

EARLIER GENERATIONS

West Africans have a long history in North America. The first Africans to arrive in what is now the United States helped to explore the New World. One well-known African explorer was Estevanico, a black African slave from Morocco. His expeditions with Álvar Núñez Cabeza de Vaca and Francisco Vázquez de Coronado in the 1500s helped establish Spain's claim to much of the Southwest. Africans also accompanied French missionaries as they moved through what is now the United States and Canada.

Millions of Slaves

For the most part, however, Africans did not come to the New World willingly. Beginning in the 1500s and continuing into the 1800s, more than 10 million West Africans

Timeline: Slavery in the United States

1619	The first slaves arrive in Jamestown, Virginia, site of the first permanent English settlement in America.
1775	The Society for the Relief of Free Negroes Unlawfully Held in Bondage, the first American organization dedicated to the **abolition** of slavery, is founded in Philadelphia.
1777	Vermont abolishes slavery. It is the first state to do so.
1793	Congress passes the Fugitive Slave Act, making it a crime to shelter runaway slaves and requiring law officers to return runaway slaves to their owners.
1808	A law forbidding the importation of slaves from Africa goes into effect. The law is poorly enforced, however, and slaves are smuggled into the United States until the 1860s.
1816	Religious leaders and slaveholders form the American Colonization Society (ACS) to return freed slaved to Africa. A few years later, former slaves settle in northwest Africa on land that eventually becomes the country of Liberia.
1831	Nat Turner, an enslaved African-American preacher, leads a slave revolt in Southampton County, Virginia. Dozens of slaveholders are killed before Turner and his followers are captured and hanged.
1839	Slaves aboard the ship *Amistad* revolt off the coast of Cuba.
1849	Harriet Tubman escapes slavery in Maryland. As one of the most effective "conductors" on the underground railroad (a secret organization that helps slaves flee to the North), she leads about three hundred slaves to freedom.
1857	In the *Dred Scott* case, the U.S. Supreme Court rules that slaves are property and are not entitled to rights under the U.S. Constitution.
1860	Abraham Lincoln is elected president.
1861	The Civil War begins.
1863	Lincoln issues the Emancipation Proclamation. It frees all slaves living in the parts of the South that are in rebellion against the United States.
1865	The Civil War ends. The Thirteenth Amendment to the U.S. Constitution abolishes slavery throughout the United States.

were taken from their homes and brought to the Americas, in chains, by European (and later also American) slave traders. Spain and then Portugal were the first European countries to begin this practice, but others soon followed. Most of these slaves were forced to work under terrible conditions in the Caribbean and Brazil.

From the early 1600s to the early 1880s, though, more than half a million West Africans were brought to what is now the United States. At first, many Africans brought to the American colonies were considered **indentured servants**. They would gain their freedom after being forced to work for a master for a period of years. But colonial laws and practices hardened over time, so that by the late 1600s, the West Africans were treated as slaves for life with no rights or liberty. Most slaves labored on the large **plantations** in the South. By the time the Civil War began in 1861, the African-American slave population of the United States was about 4 million people.

Life for African Americans under slavery could be brutal. Slave owners could work—and punish—slaves as they wished. They could buy and sell slaves as they wished,

Strike for Liberty

"Brethren, arise, arise! Strike for your lives and liberties. Now is the day and the hour. Let every slave throughout the land do this, and the days of slavery are numbered. You cannot be more oppressed than you have been—you cannot suffer greater cruelties than you have already. Rather die free men than live to be slaves. Remember that you are FOUR MILLIONS!"

With these words, Henry Highland Garnet, an escaped slave who became a prominent abolitionist, shocked people at the 1843 National Negro Convention in Buffalo, New York. His speech became known as the *Call to Rebellion*. By that time, there had been several major slave revolts. In the end, though, it would take a bloody civil war to abolish slavery in the United States.

THE BATTLE OF GETTYSBURG, PA JULY 3D 1863.

PUBLISHED BY CURRIER & IVES.

This terrific and bloody conflict between the gallant Army of the Potomac, commanded by their great General George G. Meade, and the hosts of the rebel Army of the East under General Lee; was commenced on Wednesday July 1st and ended on Friday the 3rd at 5 O'Clock P. M.— The decisive Battle was fought on Friday, ending in the complete rout & dispersion of the Rebel Army.— A Nations thanks and undying fame ever crown the Arms of the heroic soldiers, who fought with such unflinching bravery this long and desperate fight.

Almost half a million soldiers died in the Civil War before slavery was abolished throughout the United States. This painting shows some of the fierce fighting at the 1863 Battle of Gettysburg.

without regard to whether husbands and wives or parents and children were separated. Even slaves who were not treated harshly were still slaves—they were considered the property of their owners and did not have the freedom to control their own lives. Some slaves rebelled. Others ran away, often helped by abolitionists who were working to end slavery.

A House Divided

The issue of slavery divided the nation. Because the northern economy was based primarily on small family farms and handicrafts, most northern states had banned slavery by 1800. But southern states depended on large numbers of slaves to work the region's cotton, rice, tobacco, and other plantations.

The conflict over slavery was ultimately settled by the American Civil War. At the end of 1860 and early in 1861, eleven southern states seceded from the **Union**, forming the Confederate States of America (or the Confederacy), after Abraham Lincoln won the November 1860 presidential election. Lincoln had made his anti-slavery views known, but he had also said that he did not intend to interfere with slavery in the southern states where it existed. Nevertheless, most of these states saw his election as a threat to the continuation of slavery. The first shots of the Civil War were fired at Fort Sumter, South Carolina, in April 1861.

During the war, President Lincoln issued the Emancipation Proclamation. Effective January 1, 1863, this document declared all slaves free in the parts of the

This engraving shows President
Abraham Lincoln reading a draft of the
Emancipation Proclamation to his Cabinet.

Confederacy that were still in rebellion against the United States. Slaves elsewhere were not affected, including slaves in Delaware, Maryland, Missouri, and Kentucky, the so-called border states that allowed slavery but had decided to remain in the Union. As Lincoln hoped, the proclamation encouraged slaves in the Confederacy to run away, cross the front lines into Union-held territory, and volunteer to help in the North's war effort. By the time the Civil War ended in 1865, some 180,000 African Americans had served in the Union army, another 19,000 had served in the Navy, and 16 had been awarded medals of honor for their bravery in battle.

After the South was defeated and the Civil War had ended, slavery was finally prohibited throughout the United States. The Thirteenth Amendment to the U.S. Constitution, which abolished slavery nationwide, went into effect in December 1865.

Changing Times

After slavery ended, immigration from West Africa to the United States slowed to a trickle, and it remained that way for about a century. For one thing, except for Liberia, virtually all of West Africa was controlled by European colonial powers during this time. In addition, U.S. immigration laws passed in the 1920s both limited the total number of immigrants that the United States would admit each year and also favored immigrants from parts of Europe. It was not until the Immigration and Nationality Act of 1965 (which was also known as the Hart-Celler Act) was passed that

Joseph Jenkins Roberts became Liberia's first president in 1848. Born in Virginia, he went to Liberia in 1829 with his mother and two brothers.

U.S. immigration policy changed significantly. The 1965 act allowed people to enter and stay in the United States as permanent residents based largely on factors such as family connections to U.S. citizens and job skills—not country of origin.

Liberia: Land of the Free

Quakers, who were among the leading abolitionists before the Civil War, found some unlikely allies in 1816. Growing fears of slave revolts prompted several prominent slaveholders to join the Quakers in forming the American Colonization Society (ACS). The society believed that freed slaves should return to Africa—primarily because the ACS thought blacks would be unable to **assimilate** into white society. So the ACS established a colony in West Africa for former slaves.

Former slaves from Arkansas are given temporary shelter at a New York City church while waiting for a ship to take them to Liberia.

The settlement of Monrovia, named after American President James Monroe, was colonized in 1821 with the arrival of freed slaves. In 1824, the colony became known as the Republic of Liberia. During the next two decades about 19,000 former slaves moved from the United States to Liberia.

The United States and the colony of Liberia would remain closely connected. In 1847, when Liberia declared its independence, the country based its government on that of the United States. It became a model for many African colonies looking to gain independence from European colonial powers. Joseph Jenkins Roberts, a free-born African American from Virginia, became Liberia's first president.

23

Nigerian immigrants to the United States include many doctors and other highly skilled professionals.

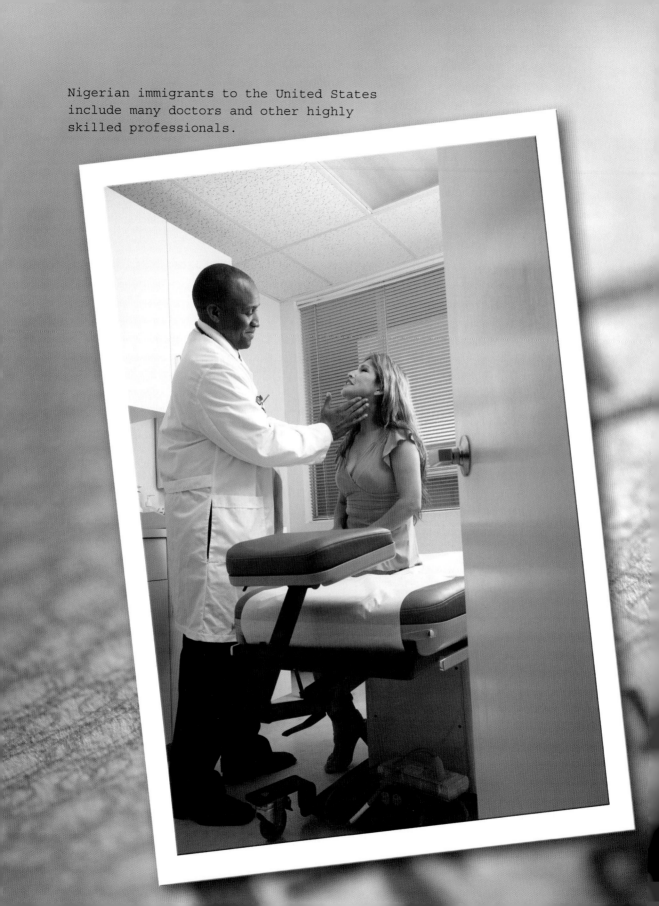

CHAPTER THREE

THE NEW IMMIGRANTS

The changes in U.S. immigration law in the 1960s occurred around the same time that a number of European colonies in West Africa gained their independence. As a result, the number of West Africans coming to the United States increased. These people included both immigrants intending to permanently relocate and students intending to stay for a few years while attending American universities.

By the 1980s, or in some cases even earlier, many young African nations were suffering both economically and politically. According to data compiled by the U.S. Immigration and Naturalization Service (renamed U.S. Citizenship and Immigration Services in 2003), the total number of African immigrants coming to the United States grew from 109,733 for the years 1961–1980 to 531,832 for the years 1981–2000. Political and economic crises in their home countries were the driving forces that prompted many West Africans, and people from other parts of Africa as well, to leave for the United States.

Ethnic and regional conflicts in Nigeria had sparked a bloody civil war that lasted from July 1967 until January 1970. Even after the fighting stopped, the country was still unstable. The military repeatedly overthrew democratically elected governments. Their hopes for the future dashed, many Nigerians left the country.

A firefight in Monrovia, Liberia's capital, in 1996 during that country's long and bloody civil war.

In a 1991 article titled "Dream or Drain?" published in *West Africa* magazine, Voice of America's Africa correspondent, James Butty, estimated that one in four African immigrants in the United States at that time had come from Nigeria. (Voice of America is a government-owned radio and television broadcasting service for foreign countries.)

During the 1980s and 1990s, civil wars erupted in a number of other West African countries. Between 1989 and 1996, about 200,000 people died in fighting between rival groups in Liberia, and more than one million Liberians became refugees. The country's historic ties made the United States a natural destination for Liberians looking to escape the fighting. In 1999, a second civil war in Liberia brought a new wave of immigrants to the United States. The war ended in 2003 when President Charles Taylor, whose tenure was marked by the murder of opposition leaders and political activists, resigned under pressure from the United States and other governments. Not all Liberians coming to the United States entered as refugees. Some arrived on work, student, or family reunification visas (the last are visas issued under the provisions of U.S. immigration law that allow citizens and permanent residents to bring immediate family members to the United States to join them). However, in 2004, Liberia was the second-leading source of refugees entering the United States (after the East African country of Somalia).

"I'm feeling like I'm going back to my country," Liberian refugee Delbora Harmon said in a 2004 interview with Voice of America. Although the Liberian-born woman had never been to the United States, like many Liberians, she felt a historic connection to the country. "Liberians were taken from America during slavery to come back home to build Liberia. And now we are the same Liberians. We are leaving again to go back to America. So, it's like we are going back to our grandparents' land."

While in power, President Taylor of Liberia supplied arms to a group called the Revolutionary United Front in neighboring Sierra Leone. In 1991, the RUF took up arms against the government of Sierra Leone's president, Joseph Momoh. In the brutal fighting that followed, the RUF kidnapped children and forced them to fight as soldiers. By the time the fighting ended in 2002, at least 50,000 people

A fourteen-year-old "child soldier" in Sierra Leone stands guard in this photo from the year 2000.

had died, thousands more had been horribly mutilated, and many more had become refugees. Several thousand of these refugees were admitted to the United States.

A military takeover of the government of Côte d'Ivoire in 1999 sparked a civil war in that country. Fighting broke out between the military and rebels, who took control of the northern part the country. Even after a peace agreement in 2003, political violence continued.

Looking Elsewhere

The civil wars and other political and economic troubles of the late twentieth and early twenty-first centuries have taken a heavy toll on West African countries, disrupting their economies, school systems, healthcare systems, and many other aspects of life. One result is that some West Africans who could afford to relocate began leaving for other countries where they could live more safely and have more opportunity. For a time, many of these people went to Europe, particularly to former colonial powers such as France and Great Britain, though some came to the United States. In the 1990s, when the U.S. economy was generally stronger than Europe's, West Africans began moving to the United States in greater numbers. These immigrants included highly educated people with sought-after professional skills, which made it easier for them to obtain visas to relocate to the United States. For example, between 1970 and 1990, 96 percent of Nigerian adults who came to the United States had college degrees. According to a World Bank report, as many as one-third of Africans

One Family's Story: Starting Over

For six years, a family of eight brothers and sisters orphaned by the civil war in Liberia lived in a refugee camp in Sierra Leone. In 2008, they started a new life in the small community of Hatfield Borough, Pennsylvania. The Lutheran Children and Family Service Refugee Resettlement Program, a local affiliate of the national Lutheran Immigration and Refugee Service, helped bring the family to the United States. The church group found the family—including twin sisters Matta and Madiafe, twenty-five; Alhaji, twenty-four; Mayamu, twenty; Mohamed, eighteen; and Mawata, also eighteen—a house on Main Street. It found jobs for the eldest at a local retirement home. The two youngest boys (their names are not used to protect their privacy), aged ten and seven, were placed with a foster family at first, but later they were allowed to live with their older brothers and sisters. Like many refugees, the family members depended on the refugee aid organization and volunteers in the community to help them get established. "The fact that they are becoming more and more self-sufficient, that's the goal," Jerry Tancredi, a member of the Lutheran refugee aid group who had been acting as a sort of guardian for the family, said in an interview with *The Reporter*, a local newspaper. "We are working with them on their checkbooks, and they are happy about getting paid and doing things on their own. It's coming along . . . nicely."

who are highly qualified professionals live abroad, most of them either in Europe or in the United States. The countries they leave behind, however, are struggling without them. In 1993 a United Nations report noted that thousands of Nigerian-born doctors were practicing in the United States, while Nigeria was suffering from a shortage of doctors.

By the 1990s, increasing numbers of West Africans who first came to the United States as students were choosing to remain in the country after they graduated. According to the Institute of International Education, which keeps statistics on foreigners studying in the United States, seventeen to eighteen thousand Africans—most of them from English-speaking countries in West Africa—attended

U.S. universities and colleges each year during the 1990s. Since 2001, that number has jumped to at least thirty thousand a year. Many African students who earned degrees then sought out U.S. employers to sponsor them as permanent residents. The employers apply for permanent resident visas for the students.

Winning the Lottery

In 1990, the U.S. government set up the Diversity Visa Program. This program has helped people in Asia and Africa who wish to immigrate to the United States. The program distributes fifty thousand permanent resident visas each year via lottery (random selection) to people from countries with historically low rates of immigration to the United States. Generally, far more people apply each year than the number of visas available. To win the lottery, besides having some luck, applicants have to show that they qualify for a visa. That means they must have no criminal record, be healthy, and have at least a high school education. About 40 percent of the diversity visas go to Africans. Since 1990, hundreds of thousands of African immigrants have been able to come to the United States through this lottery.

Those who receive permanent resident visas, whether through the lottery program or otherwise, can then sponsor close relatives to join them in the United States under the U.S. family reunification program. This allows a further increase in the total number of immigrants. Created under the Immigration and Nationality Act of 1965, the family reunification program allows immigrants who are permanent residents and U.S. citizens to send for spouses and children under eighteen (citizens can send for other close family members as well and face no numerical limits on the number of such family members they can bring to join them in the United States).

Challenges for Refugees from West Africa

About one-third of recent arrivals from Africa are refugees. Their situation sets them apart from other immigrants in several important ways. Unlike people who choose to leave their home countries, refugees have been forced to leave. They may have witnessed horrifying violence and only narrowly escaped with little more than the clothes on their backs. As a result, they are typically poorer than West African immigrants who choose to move to the United States. Some, having endured civil wars and years of living in refugee camps, may be less well-educated than the average immigrant from West Africa.

Because refugees are forced to leave family members—and sometimes houses and businesses—behind, many stay in close contact with their home countries. In the United States, they often become part of cultural organizations founded by other immigrants, such as the Organization of Nigerian Citizens. Founded in 1986 in Maryland, the organization now has chapters in more than twenty states. Within such groups, the new immigrants work to raise awareness of the problems that forced them to leave. Many work from afar to bring about political changes so they can return home.

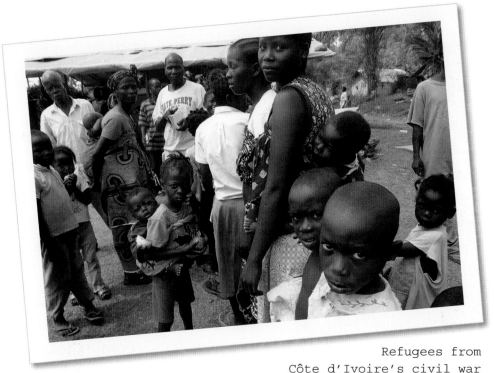

Refugees from
Côte d'Ivoire's civil war
line up at a United Nations refugee camp in 2002.

In 1997, 6,000 African refugees entered the United States. That's a small number compared with the 48,000 European refugees who entered that same year. The Congressional Black Caucus, a group consisting of African-American members of the U.S. Congress, expressed concern that refugee programs **discriminated** against Africans. In 1999, President Bill Clinton raised the number of African refugees to be admitted each year to 12,000. In 2000, the limit was raised again, this time to 18,000.

Immigration policy changed after terrorists attacked the United States on September 11, 2001. In March 2003, the newly formed Department of Homeland Security was placed in charge of many aspects of immigration. The refugee resettlement program was temporarily suspended.

When it resumed, the number of refugees from all countries being admitted to the United States was much lower than it had been in previous years. U.S. immigration officials who once processed refugees were instead told to focus on border security. With additional security checks and fewer immigration officials to deal with refugees, the resettlement process became painfully slow, leaving thousands of West Africans stranded in refugee camps.

In 2003, the International Rescue Committee, a refugee resettlement agency, estimated that refugees from Sierra Leone waited an average of five years to enter the United States. Liberian refugees waited an average of seven years. That was the case even for refugees who had family members in the United States and were eligible for admission under the family reunification program.

Some African immigrants blame **racism** for delays in processing refugees. After 2001, immigration processing at refugee camps resumed elsewhere in the world before it did in Africa. "I can't understand why only in Africa is there a problem bringing refugees here," said Maphata Roberts at a refugee fundraising event held in California in 2003. Roberts, a Liberian-born U.S. citizen, had been trying to bring her family to the United States from a refugee camp in Ghana for ten years. "We pay our taxes, and we do everything we can like all other citizens. . . . Africa suffers because—maybe because we're black?"

The length of time people wait to gain admittance to the United States remains long, but in recent years the number of African refugees allowed into the country has increased.

The U.S. government acted, for example, to admit a greater number of Liberian refugees. Between 2003 and 2005, the U.S. Refugee Program helped more than eight thousand Liberian refugees resettle in the United States. "Our children have not been to school for almost ten years. We've been promised work and lodging in the U.S., and we can't wait for our departure day," said Amos Dagbe in an interview with the news agency *Reuters* in 2004. The father of six had fled Liberia with his family in the 1990s.

The Department of Homeland Security reported that 22,000 African refugees came to the United States in 2007. Additionally, there were about 3,600 Liberians living in the United States under Temporary Protected Status (TPS). The U.S. government grants TPS to people who cannot safely return to their home countries. It allows them to stay in the United States for a set period of time without documentation. Political and economic conditions in Liberia began to improve following the 2005 presidential election there. However, the country remained unstable enough that, in 2007, President George W. Bush extended the Temporary Protected Status for Liberians.

East Meets West in Texas

Many recent African refugees have settled in Dallas, Texas. By some estimates, by 2008, the city was home to more than a hundred thousand immigrants from twenty African countries. The majority of them come from West Africa, and Nigerians represent the largest group from one country. Many of these Nigerian Americans are doctors, lawyers,

The Dallas area has a large West African immigrant community, including these sisters looking at children's art at a gallery in the city.

and engineers who began coming to Texas in the 1970s. The large number of Africans already in Dallas makes it a natural destination for new immigrants. However, a number of the newest arrivals come from East Africa or Central Africa, and they have little in common with the more established immigrant groups. In addition to coming from different countries, they speak different languages and belong to different ethnic groups. Their only common ground is that they were forced to leave their home countries and are starting over in the United States. Among the newcomers are about 750 people from Burundi, who arrived from refugee camps in Tanzania in 2007 and 2008, and 400 people from Sudan. "We are not united," Sethi Bigirimana, a Burundian refugee, told a reporter for the *Dallas Morning News* in June 2008. "We are taught East and West don't go. It's tradition and unnatural to crack that."

Though some Americans may think of all immigrants from Africa as a single group, the cultural and ethnic difference between people from different countries (or even different parts of the same country) are real, and they can be significant.

The Center for Families, started in 2006 by the Greater Minneapolis Council of Churches, was set up in part to provide help to recent West African immigrants in finding housing, getting healthcare, and finding jobs. But another one of its goals was to bring together people from different countries of origin to reduce tensions and increase cooperation within the West African immigrant community.

The *Dallas Morning News* reporter who interviewed Sethi Bigirimana also spoke with Alusine Jalloh, an immigrant from Sierra Leone and an associate professor of history at the University of Texas at Arlington. Jalloh was also the director of the university's Africa Program, an organization he established in 1992 to promote business, educational, and technological connections between Texas and Africa. "We are starting to see partnerships between universities and churches in the African community in raising awareness about challenges here and [in Africa] like droughts and civil war," he said. "But we are not there yet in terms of a common identity. I always tell my students when the chips are down, Africans think ethnically."

Malian-American sculptor Ibou N'Diaye
in his Pittsburgh studio with one of
his unfinished works.

CHAPTER FOUR

MAKING A NEW LIFE

West Africans often arrive in the United States with unrealistic expectations of what life will be like in their adopted country. In an interview with National Public Radio (NPR), Sidi Ibrahime, an immigrant from Côte d'Ivoire, said that American television and movies have convinced some immigrants that it's much easier than it really is to make a lot of money in the United States. Ibrahime, who worked as a taxi driver in New York City, was featured in *Dollars and Dreams: West Africans in New York*, a **documentary** film produced in 2007 by independent filmmakers Jeremy Rocklin and Abdel Kader Ouedraogo. The film aims, in part, to give immigrants from Africa a truer picture of the challenges they face.

Unlike an idealized Hollywood version of the immigrant experience, West African immigrants in the United States often face racial and religious discrimination. Many West Africans are Muslims—that is, they are followers of the religion of Islam. Because the men who carried out the September 11, 2001, terrorist attacks were Islamic **extremists**, the attacks led to increased **prejudice** against—and fear of—Muslims on the part of some Americans.

Some West African immigrants find themselves facing prejudice based on race for the first time. Because most residents of West Africa are black, racism is rarely an issue there. In a 1999 interview with the *New York Times*, Tingah Mohammed, a forty-nine-year-old from Ghana, said he had never heard of racism until he came to the United States in the early 1980s.

Education Is Key

Although West African immigrants are, as a group, highly educated, some immigrants are unable, at least at first, to duplicate the occupational success they had in Africa. An engineer from Nigeria, for example, may end up working as a waiter or a cook in a restaurant, at least for a while, because his professional credentials are not accepted in the United States. (In order to practice many professions in the United States, it is necessary to obtain a certificate or license from a professional association or government agency, and sometimes to pass an exam.) West Africans from French-speaking countries often struggle to overcome language barriers. Even those immigrants who are from

A Liberian immigrant
tutors his daughter and other immigrant
children at an after-school program in New York City.

English-speaking countries in West Africa find that many Americans—including potential employers—have a hard time understanding their accents.

Still, the median family income for African-born immigrants was $40,000 in 2003, only about $4,000 less than the median income for all Americans, and many make much more than that. Among Nigerian Americans in 2006, the median family income was more than $62,000, almost $4,000 higher than the figure for all American families that year. Additionally, compared with other immigrant groups, West Africans are less likely to work in service, production, transportation, or agricultural jobs (all of which tend to be lower paying).

Many West African immigrants become **entrepreneurs** and open their own businesses, including restaurants, groceries, and specialty stores that cater to the needs of other West African immigrants. In such New York City neighborhoods as Greenwich Village, Bedford-Stuyvesant, and Harlem, food markets feature sweet **plantain** chips, smoked beef, kola nuts, and Ghanaian peanut soup, and clothing stores sell dashiki shirts and colorful, handmade items.

In addition, West African street vendors set up shop on many street corners. These vendors include some undocumented immigrants who may have entered the United States on short-term tourist visas and then simply stayed. A number of former French colonies in West Africa share the same currency. After that currency dropped sharply in value in the mid–1990s, creating an economic crisis, immigration to the United States (both documented and undocumented) increased from Senegal and from other French-speaking African countries. The street vendors form part of the "underground economy"—buying and selling for cash only and avoiding any contact with government agencies. Although the vendors are concentrated in larger cities, such as New York, some make trips to other parts of the United States to sell their wares at African festivals or markets (trips that the vendors refer to informally as "going into the bush").

In recent years, the Washington, D.C., area has become a magnet for West African immigrants. In general, those who live in Washington make more money and are better educated than African immigrants who settle elsewhere in

Shots Heard Around the World

At 12:40 A.M. on February 4, 1999, four New York City police officers approached Amadou Diallo, a twenty-two-year-old immigrant from the West African country of Guinea, as he stood in front of his apartment building in the Bronx. The police officers, all of whom were white and who were wearing street clothes, later said that they thought Diallo resembled a criminal they had been looking for and that they wanted to question him. When Diallo put his hand in his jacket pocket, the police, thinking he was reaching for a gun, fired forty-one shots at him, hitting him nineteen times. It turned out that Diallo, who was unarmed, was trying to pull out his wallet, presumably to show the officers some form of identification.

Marchers protest the shooting of Amadou Diallo by New York City police officers. Diallo's father is second from the right.

Diallo's death sparked many protests in New York City and elsewhere against certain police tactics, especially alleged racial profiling—the practice of considering race when determining whether a person is likely to have committed a crime or is likely to pose a threat. There were also questions about the justification for firing at the suspect a total of forty-one times. The shooting left many immigrants feeling afraid. Silla Sidique, a thirty-five-year-old Guinean businessman, had been in the United States for just a year when the shooting happened. "I want to go back before somebody kills me," he told a *New York Times* reporter.

A similar incident occurred in 2003 when a New York City police officer shot a forty-two-year-old West African immigrant from Burkina Faso. The immigrant, named Ousmane Zongo, kept and repaired African art objects at a warehouse that the police were guarding in the hope of catching people who were marketing counterfeit compact discs. The police officer later testified that Zongo ignored his order to drop to the ground and that Zongo tried to grab the officer's gun. The officer shot Zongo four times. Like Diallo, Zongo was unarmed and had no criminal record.

The Diallo and Zongo families both filed lawsuits against the City of New York and the police officers involved, and each family was awarded about $3 million.

43

the United States. In 2005, for instance, the median house-hold income for African-born people living in the Washington area was about $53,000. About 43 percent of them had college degrees. More than a third worked as professionals (doctors, lawyers, and the like), in management, or in office jobs.

Culture Clashes

Sam Uzoh, a Nigerian immigrant living in Houston, Texas, opened two stores selling African art, clothing, music, and films. With more than 20,000 African immigrants living in the Houston area, he had no shortage of customers. His stores also attracted many African Americans who wanted to learn more about their heritage.

In a 2005 interview with Voice of America, though, Uzoh said he was troubled by the number of people who asked him if anything good happens in Africa. Uzoh said many people associate Africa only with war and starvation. To try to balance those images, he started importing movies, many of which are made in Nigeria, to sell in his stores. The African-made films, he said, educate and entertain his customers and provide them with a more balanced view of West African life.

At the same time, learning about West African culture, which differs from U.S. culture in significant ways, can go a long way toward reducing misunderstandings. In Mauritania, for instance, it is socially unacceptable for men to take money from women. So when an immigrant from Mauritania was working as a busboy in a New York

This West African immigrant in New York left her husband when he took a second wife.

restaurant, he refused to take his share of the waitresses' tips. In response, the restaurant's management gave the busboy's share of the tips to a male employee, who then passed the money along to the busboy.

Another American–West African culture clash involves the institution of marriage. In many West African countries, it is both legal and acceptable for a man to have more than one wife. This practice, called **polygamy**, is illegal in the United States. Immigration officials won't give visas to men who are in polygamous marriages. Still, some West African immigrants continue the practice in secret.

"It's difficult, but one accepts it because it's our religion," said Doussou Traore, a Muslim and president of a New York association of Malian women (in Mali, about four out of every ten married women are in polygamous marriages). In an

interview with the *New York Times*, Traore said her husband
had two other wives in Mali. "Our mothers accepted it. Our
grandmothers accepted it," she said. "Why not us?"

A Guinean-born businesswoman presented the issue in
a much harsher light. "The woman is in effect the slave of
the man," she said in the *New York Times* article. "If you
protest, your husband will hit you, and if you call the police, he's going to divorce you, and the whole community
will scorn you." Some West African immigrant women
take that risk and leave. Others stay with their husbands
because they fear they will be **deported** (sent back to their
home countries) if they contact authorities or try to leave
the household.

Many West Africans are more concerned about family
separation than about polygamy. Some West African men
come to the United States alone, to find work. Because they
send much of their income to relatives they left behind—
African immigrants send about $3 billion to Africa each
year—some may be unable to save enough to pay for visas
and airfare so that their family members can join them.

In recent years, a growing number of West African
women, many of them single, are choosing to immigrate
to the United States alone in search of better economic
opportunity. This is often an act of courage for women
brought up in traditionally male-dominated societies in
which the woman's role is considered to be in the home. In
immigrant communities in New York and other major cities, West African women are starting their own businesses,
including hair salons featuring braiding and other West

African styles and restaurants serving West African dishes. Khadija Sow, an immigrant from Senegal, opened a restaurant in the Bedford-Stuyvesant neighborhood of Brooklyn, New York. "Our traditional cuisine is in high demand among single African males who were brought up with the idea that a man's place is not in a kitchen," Sow told an interviewer for the online publication *Women's eNews* in 2002. "They don't even know how to cook an egg, and therefore order daily from places like mine." Sow said that most of her customers were men.

A Lonely Life

Overall, West African immigrants are less likely than newcomers from other regions of the world to live in immigrant communities. West African immigrants are scattered across the United States. Far from home, and cut off from other people who have similar backgrounds and experiences, some find that life in the United States can be lonely.

Ibou N'Diaye, an artist from Mali, met his American-born wife while she was working in Mali as a Peace Corps volunteer. In the early 2000s, the couple lived in Pittsburgh, Pennsylvania, with their son. In an interview with the *Pittsburgh Post-Gazette* in 2003, N'Daiye talked about the differences between life in his tight-knit Mali community and in the United States. In Mali, he said, "Every morning, I wake up, I'm surrounded by friends. A lot of people come, we drink tea, we play music. More than twenty people come in the studio every day." In the United States, he said, "I wake up, all the day I am alone."

Professor Jean-Jacques Sene uses a map of Africa in the fifteenth century in one of his history classes.

Jean-Jacques Sene, a professor of African history who grew up in a small community in Senegal, understands. "In African families, the home was an open place," he told the *Pittsburgh Post-Gazette* reporter. "Family and friends just dropped in. Living in the West, you have to call or schedule before you visit."

Some West African immigrants have responded by creating new support networks. Some belong to organizations that bring immigrants from the same country together for traditional meals and celebrations. These groups also raise money for people and causes that are important to members. For immigrants, it's a way to stay close to home.

African-American Tensions

Some West African immigrants are drawn to African-American neighborhoods in New York, Atlanta, Philadelphia, and other large cities. There, they are less likely to encounter racism, but they still may have to deal with anti-immigrant attitudes. As the number of immigrants has risen, so have tensions between African-born immigrants and African Americans whose ancestors have been in the United States for generations.

Some American-born blacks welcome the immigrants, and they see the West African restaurants, stores, and cultural organizations that the recent arrivals open as neighborhood improvements and opportunities to learn more about their cultural heritage. But other African Americans see the newcomers as competition for jobs, and they complain that West African immigrants are benefiting from programs that were designed to benefit African Americans. For instance, some say West African immigrants are taking places in U.S. universities that would have been filled by African Americans under affirmative action programs (that is, programs undertaken to increase educational and employment opportunities for groups that had long been discriminated against).

Studies show that foreign-born blacks are less likely to be poor or unemployed than African Americans. Some American-born blacks resent the immigrants' success. Tensions between African Americans and West African immigrants flared in Philadelphia in 2005 when a thirteen-year-old Liberian-born boy was beaten by a group of African-American students. "The [immigrant] kids talk about being [made fun of and] sometimes being told to go back to Africa," said Liberian-born Portia Kamara, director of Multicultural Family Services, a social services agency in Philadelphia.

African-born and American-born blacks are working hard to bridge the culture gaps in their communities. Although the groups have different histories, their experiences are similar.

Just as African Americans struggled to overcome slavery and racism in the United States, West Africans struggled against the economic and social consequences of colonialism, a system in which militarily strong nations established control over weaker nations. Both fought hard to win their freedom and their civil rights. In Philadelphia, community leaders are creating community-based cultural exchange programs to help African Americans and West Africans get to know each other better. Some of these programs include cultural sensitivity training for police and local social service organizations. Others are more celebratory. Odunde is a Yoruba festival organized by African Americans in Philadelphia that attracts many African immigrants. Groups such as the Philadelphia Folklore Project run programs such as Philly Dance Africa to bring African Americans and African immigrants together for performances.

Caught in the Middle

Children of West African immigrants often adapt more easily than their parents to life in the United States. But, like most immigrants, West African parents don't want their children to forget their heritage or forget their traditional cultural values.

"African parents feel their children are being influenced," Orabella Richards, a Liberian-born businesswoman in Philadelphia said in an interview for *FrontPageAfrica.com*, an Internet publication based in the United States that focuses on news from Africa, particularly Liberia. "The kids assimilate. They try and imitate [African-American] children in their manner, their dress. They're hanging out in the neighborhood. And their parents don't want that."

West African parents believe in strict discipline, and children are taught to respect their elders. American children are often allowed more freedom than African children traditionally are allowed. "It takes a village to raise a child" is a popular African saying, and in West Africa, large extended families in tight-knit communities do indeed share the responsibility for raising children. In the United States, parents generally are expected to raise children on their own.

Ultimately, most West Africans are as eager as other immigrants to assimilate into the larger American community, and they're grateful when their American-born peers offer a helping hand. Freddy Adu, an immigrant from Ghana who in 2003 became the United States' youngest professional soccer player, entered the United States in 1997 when his mother obtained a visa through the Diversity Visa Program lottery. The family settled in Potomac, Maryland, a Washington, D.C., suburb, where life was very different from life in Ghana. Adu adjusted quickly, though. "When I started school, my classmates accepted me . . . and helped me through everything. I didn't know the language [English] that well—and the slang— but they helped me. It made everything easier," Adu said in a 2005 interview with *eJournal USA*, a publication of the U.S. Department of State's Bureau of International Information Programs. "The kids were . . . intrigued by me. Here comes a kid from Africa—they weren't used to that. They were drawn to me and asked a lot of questions. That definitely helped my relationship with them."

West African musicians perform in
Portland, Oregon, at the Homowo
Festival, a traditional celebration
of the Ga people of Ghana.

CHAPTER FIVE

10 MAY 1999

CHANGING THE AMERICAN CULTURE

Although many West Africans are fairly recent immigrants, they are making their presence felt. In addition to Philadelphia, New York, and Washington, D.C., African markets have sprung up in Saint Paul, Minnesota; Tucson, Arizona; Annapolis, Maryland; and other cities. West African drumming and dance troupes perform across the United States. One such troupe is Zadonu, a California-based company founded by Ghanaian-American musicians and teachers Kobla and Dzidzorgbe Ladzekpo. In addition to performing, members of Zadonu hold workshops and seminars on African culture.

West African Americans are proud of their cultural heritage. Even longtime U.S. residents still listen to

Descendants of the Gullah
people of West Africa, brought to the
South as slaves, still carry on their traditions,
as shown by this woman weaving baskets in South Carolina.

West-African music, eat West-African foods, and participate in traditional African festivals. For example, in New York City; Philadelphia; Portland, Oregon; and other communities, Ghanaian Americans join in the Homowo Festival, a traditional celebration of the Ga people of Ghana. The festival includes African foods, dancing, music, and storytelling. Its purpose is to give thanks to ancestors and spirits.

Some immigrants from Africa stand out in a crowd because they wear traditional African clothes. Kente cloth, for instance, is a popular West-African fabric. The name comes from the word *kenten*, which means "basket." Once known as the "cloth of kings" because it was worn by Ghanaian royalty, the cloth has patterns that are similar to the woven designs of baskets. Each pattern has a special name and meaning. Many patterns are associated with particular ethnic groups.

On such special occasions as National Day (October 1), when Nigerians celebrate their independence from British colonial rule, some Nigerian-American men wear long, flowing robes called *agbadas*, and women wear traditional head scarves and thin veils.

What's the Word?

Although two-thirds of African-born Americans speak English, in 2005 only 17 percent said they spoke English at home. Most spoke African languages at home, although about 14 percent (especially immigrants from onetime French colonies such as Senegal, Guinea, Mali, and Côte d'Ivoire) spoke French. Many West Africans also speak pidgin English, which is a mixture of English and one or more other languages. When used by Africans, pidgin grammar and vocabulary are closer to African languages than to English. The words have their roots in English, but they are pronounced differently and put together differently in sentences. For instance, "Man wey fool na him loss" is a Nigerian proverb in pidgin English. It means: "It is the fool that loses." Another Nigerian proverb—"Monkey no fine but im mamma like am so"—means "The monkey may not look handsome, but his mother likes him as he is."

Pidgin English can be difficult for Americans to understand. But for one group of people in the South, it's almost a mother tongue. The Gullah people are the descendants of slaves from West Africa. Researchers think the name Gullah may come from Gola, the name of a small tribe on the border of present-day Sierra Leone and Liberia. The Vai (also known as Gallinas or Galo), Mende, and Kissi people also live in the same region.

The Gullah were brought to the United States to work on the rice plantations of the coastal regions of South Carolina and Georgia. Malaria, yellow fever, and other tropical diseases were common in these swampy areas. The West Africans came from tropical climates and had some resistance to those diseases. The white settlers did not. During the humid summer months when the threat of disease was highest, most slave owners went elsewhere and left the slaves to run the plantations.

Typically, West African slaves were forced to abandon their traditions. The Gullah people, however, because they lived in isolation, were able to continue their traditional cultural practices. They cooked West African dishes, entertained their children with folktales, practiced traditional religions, and wove baskets with tribal designs. Over time, the West African Krio language spoken by the Gullah mixed with English to create a type of pidgin tongue called Creole. (Other forms of Creole, especially those spoken in Louisiana, contain more French than English.)

After the Civil War, competition from plantations in Louisiana, Arkansas, and Texas put many South Carolina and Georgia rice plantations out of business. Plantation owners abandoned the area, but the Gullah people stayed on. They continue their traditional way of life to this day.

The Past Shapes the Future

Political difficulties in West Africa as well as U.S. economic

Characters from African Folklore

Many American children grow up hearing African folk tales, especially the Uncle Remus tales of human-like animals named Brer Rabbit, Brer Fox, Brer Bear, and Brer Snake. These stories were collected and published in book form more than a century ago by Joel Chandler Harris (1845–1908), a white man who heard the stories from the Gullah people in his home state of Georgia. The stories are traditional folktales that originated in West Africa. *Brer* is a shortened form of the word "brother."

Brer Rabbit, a trickster character who always outsmarts his enemies, is based on a character known as Koni Rabbit in Sierra Leone. African folktales are full of tricksters. The most famous is Anansi the Spider, who appears in folktales told by the Mende, Temne, and Limba people.

In 1946, Walt Disney used Chandler's stories as the basis of a film called *Song of the South*. Sixty year later, in 2006, Universal released *The Adventures of Brer Rabbit*, an animated children's movie, on DVD. The cartoon character Bugs Bunny is a modern-day version of the trickster: He's smart and he doesn't always play fair.

opportunities combined to bring some of the best and brightest people from West Africa to the United States. Computer scientist Philip Emeagwali, for one, was born in Nigeria in 1954 and came to the United States initially to attend Oregon State University on a full scholarship when he was seventeen. In 1989, Emeagwali won the Institute of Electrical and Electronics Engineers' Gordon Bell Prize for his work on a series of **supercomputers** called the Connection Machine. He has won more than one hundred professional awards since then.

In addition to the many West African-born engineers, scientists, doctors, and businesspeople who now live in the United States, West African-born writers, artists, musicians, and filmmakers are expanding Americans' understanding of West African culture. Nigerian-born writers Chinua

Achebe and Akin Adesokan both teach at U.S. universities. The famed Nigerian-born drummer, educator, and social activist Babatunde Olatunji (1927–2003) also made his home in the United States.

Popular Culture

Turn on the television, and you'll see West African Americans popping up all over the place. Gbenga Akinnagbe, the American-born son of Nigerian parents, became one of the stars of the HBO police drama *The Wire*. Nigerian-American

Liberian-American fashion designer Korto Momolu *(center)* works with models before a show in New York.

singer Chikezie Eze, who was born in California, was a top contender on *American Idol* in 2008. Liberian-born fashion designer Korto Momolu was a finalist on the 2008 season of *Project Runway*, a television show in which **aspiring** clothing designers compete with each other.

Things Fall Apart

Chinua Achebe, one of the best-known authors to come out of West Africa, was born in the Nigerian village of Nneobi in 1930. His first novel, *Things Fall Apart*, was published in 1958. The story of a Nigerian warrior who is unable to adapt to changing conditions after the British colonization of Nigeria, it sold more than 8 million copies, making it one of the most widely read books in modern African literature. Achebe has also written several other novels, as well as short stories, poetry, essays, and children's books. Many of his works focus on the Igbo people of Nigeria and the clash of cultures that occurred during the colonial era.

Achebe was active in Nigerian politics. In 1967, the Biafra region of Nigeria broke away from the country and declared its independence. The split caused a bloody civil war. In 1970, Nigeria reclaimed the region. Achebe, who favored Biafran independence, became disheartened, and in 1972, he moved to the United States. He returned to Nigeria in 1976, but came back to the United States in 1990 after a car accident left him paralyzed from the waist down. Since 1990, he has been a professor of languages and literature at Bard College in New York State.

Nigerian-born author Chinua Achebe at his home on the campus of Bard College in New York.

Nigerian-American singer Titilayo Rachel Adedokun in a performance of the opera *Aida*.

She didn't win, but the show created several opportunities for her.

"I was invited by the president of Liberia, where I'm from, to go back to Liberia . . . and I'm going to design a gown for her and be featured in this women's conference," Korto said in a 2008 interview with the magazine *Entertainment Weekly*. "So from the show, I'm able to go home after seventeen years, to be invited by my president, that's an amazing honor. I'm so excited about that."

American performers of Nigerian descent include the poet and singer Iyeoka Ivie Okoawo and the rapper Wale Folarin, better known simply as Wale. Singer Titilayo Rachel Adedokun, born in Nashville, Tennessee, to parents of

Goooaaaal!!!

In Ghana, where he was born in 1989, Freddy Adu loved playing soccer barefoot with friends. He always dreamed of playing professional soccer. After his family moved to Maryland in 1997, he was determined to make his dream come true. When he was twelve, Adu enrolled at the IMG Soccer Academy, a full-time training program in Florida run by the United States Soccer Federation. In November 2003, the left-footed midfielder signed a $500,000 contract to play for the major league soccer team D.C. United—making him, at age fourteen, the youngest American athlete to turn pro since fourteen-year-old Fred Chapman played major league baseball in 1887.

Soccer observers expected a lot from Adu; some even compared him to Pele, considered by many to be the greatest soccer player of all time. At first, Adu struggled under the pressure to succeed.

In 2007, however, he was in top form playing for the U.S. team in the Fédération Internationale de Football Association (International Federation of Association Football) U-20 World Cup in Canada. His performance in that tournament—the soccer world championship for male players under twenty years old—landed him a contract with Benfica, one of Portugal's top soccer teams. In 2008, Adu played on the U.S. team in the Beijing Olympics. That same year, he joined the European team AS Monaco.

Freddy Adu in action during a 2008 game.

Nigerian origin, was Miss Ohio and second runner-up in the 1994 Miss America pageant. In 2009 she was living in Germany and performing in operas, musical comedies, and jazz clubs all over the world.

A Sporting Chance

West Africans have become stars in major American sports leagues. Nigerian-born National Basketball Association superstar Hakeem Olajuwon, nicknamed Hakeem the Dream, led the Houston Rockets to NBA championship in 1994 and 1995. The National Football League in 2008 boasted a number of Nigerian-born players or players of Nigerian descent, including Amobi Okoye (Houston Texans), Israel Idonije (Chicago Bears), and Adewale Ogunleye (Chicago Bears).

Okoye was twelve when he left Nigeria to come to the United States. Yet, like many West African immigrants, he hasn't lost sight of where he came from and how much his country needs his help. In 2008, Okoye, Idonije, and Ogunleye traveled to Nigeria as "Nigerian NFL ambassadors." The football stars established scholarships at Nigerian universities, distributed materials to test for the human immunodeficiency virus (HIV—the virus that causes AIDS), and gave soccer equipment to local youths. (Soccer, known as football outside the United States, is the most popular sport in Nigeria. Okoye had never played American football until he moved to the United States.) "It was overwhelming what needs to be done there," Okoye said. "There are so many needs in Nigeria. That's why we planned this trip."

Many people in Africa celebrated when Barack
Obama, whose father was an immigrant from
the African country of Kenya, was elected
president of the United States in 2008.

CHAPTER SIX

LOOKING TO THE FUTURE

Skilled and determined, immigrants from West Africa are among the highest achieving newcomers to the United States. That success hasn't always meant that they have fully integrated into American society, however. Most West African immigrants are still closely connected to their native countries. They are culturally very different from African Americans whose ancestors arrived as slaves, and they are not always comfortable in white America. Nevertheless, the 2008 election results provided evidence that racial and cultural divides in the United States may be narrowing.

Voting For Change

Until recently, few West African Americans had been politically active in the United States. But in 2008, with Barack

Just decades before Obama's election, U.S. Army troops had to protect African-American students starting to attend formerly all-white schools in the South. The scene here is at Little Rock High School in Arkansas in 1957. Many people saw Obama's election as a sign of improved race relations in the United States.

Obama on the ballot as the Democratic candidate for president, many West African Americans eligible to vote were inspired to vote in a U.S. election for the first time. Children of immigrants, in particular, may have found that Obama's experiences in the United States echoed their own.

The son of a Kenyan-born man and an American woman from Kansas, Obama was born in Hawaii in 1961. His father was part of the wave of Africans who came to study in the United States in the 1960s. Like many children born to African immigrants, Obama found himself torn between different cultures. Although he has relatives in Kenya (which is in East Africa), he was mostly raised by his white mother and her parents in the United States.

Obama's cultural identity became an issue during the 2008 presidential campaign. Unlike the ancestors of most African Americans, Obama's ancestors weren't slaves. He is too young to have taken part in the struggles of the U.S. civil rights movement of the 1950s and 1960s, to attain greater rights for black Americans. Obama himself went to Columbia University in New York City and Harvard Law School in Cambridge, Massachusetts, and worked as a civil rights lawyer in Chicago before becoming a U.S. senator from Illinois in 2004. Some political and social scientists have said that Obama's cultural history set him apart from the established African-American community. Others have said his race set him apart from the larger white community. His father's immigrant background and the fact that Obama lived abroad in Indonesia as a child led some voters to question his "American-ness" and even his patriotism.

Although Obama was raised as a Christian, the facts that his father was a Muslim and that his middle name is Hussein caused some voters to assume he was a Muslim and to say they would not vote for him on that basis—much to the distress of West African Americans, many of whom are Muslim.

On Election Day, U.S. citizens turned out to vote in near record numbers. Despite the concerns—and prejudices—of some voters, Obama won by a comfortable margin. He made history by becoming the first African American to be elected president of the United States. Many people saw Obama's win as a major, if far from final, victory over the racism of the past in the United States.

High Hopes

Obama's election also brought new hope to West African immigrants. Many were optimistic that his personal connections to Africa would lead the United States to focus more on the continent's problems. Obama addressed these problems in his 2006 book *The Audacity of Hope: Thoughts on Reclaiming the American Dream*: "There are times when considering the plight of Africa—the millions racked by AIDS, the constant droughts and famines, the dictatorships, the pervasive corruption, the brutality of twelve-year-old guerrillas [rebel fighters] who know nothing but war wielding machetes or AK-47s [automatic rifles]—I find myself plunged into cynicism and despair."

The book also talked of the progress Africa has made. "There are positive trends in Africa often hidden in the

Although much of the news from West Africa focuses on the region's problems, many West Africans enjoy life in modern cities. Shown here: Lagos, the largest city in Nigeria.

news of despair," Obama wrote in *The Audacity of Hope*. "Democracy is spreading. In many places economies are growing. We need to build on these glimmers of hope and help those committed leaders and citizens throughout Africa build the better future they, like we, so desperately desire."

Improving conditions in West Africa may result in fewer immigrants coming to the United States. If the political and economic situations get better, some immigrants might also be drawn back to their home countries. It takes both talent and hard work to succeed in the United States, West African immigrant Sidi Ibrahime said in an interview with National Public Radio. But he also noted that those same qualities would bring equal success in his home country of Côte d'Ivoire. Some West Africans who came to the United States as refugees dream of being able to return home to Africa once their native countries are politically and economically stable.

Lowering Immigration Barriers

Many West African Americans said that immigration reform was the biggest issue for them in the 2008 election. As the son of an immigrant, Obama seemed to be listening. During his presidential campaign, he said, "We've got to fix a broken immigration system not just for the undocumented but for legal immigrants. The backlogs are horrendous. The fees have been increased and doubled and tripled. As a consequence, more and more people are having difficulty just trying to reunify their families, even if they're going through the legal pathways. And that puts more pressure on people to go into the illegal system."

The president, after consulting with Congress, has the power to decide how many refugees will be admitted to the United States yearly from each region of the world. West African immigrants with family members stuck in refugee

During the 2008 campaign,
Obama (*shown here on election night*)
spoke of reforming U.S. immigration policy to reduce
the delays for immigrants trying to obtain visas.

camps advocate an increase in the number of African
refugees allowed into the United States.

An Immigrant's Dream

West Africans place a high value on education. Most West
African immigrants in the United States intend to send
their children to college. That bodes well for their future
in the United States. For many West Africans, Obama's

71

Nigerian Americans, sometimes wearing the traditional clothing of their native country, are a part of twenty-first century American life.

success represented a realization of the immigrant dream. On election night 2008, a group of West Africans gathered to watch the results at the Majestic Lounge in Sacramento, California. The nightclub and restaurant's owner is Gregoire Tonoukouin, who had come to the United States from the West African country of Benin.

"We are so many Obamas in America, but he really stands out," Tonoukouin said in an interview with the *Sacramento Bee* newspaper. "So educated, such good family values. We know now, we immigrants and our children, that we can do everything."

FACTS ABOUT NIGERIAN AMERICANS

Characteristic	Nigerian Americans	Percentage for Nigerian Americans	Total U.S. Population	Percentage for U.S. Population
Total population	237,527		299,398,485	
Male	130,640	55%	146,705,258	49%
Female	106,887	45%	152,693,227	51%
Median age (years)	29		36	
Under 5 years old	17, 270	11%	20,957,894	7%
18 years and over	107,753	68%	224,548,864	75%
65 years and over	2,520	2%	35,927,818	12%
Average family size	4		3	
Number of households	76,222		111,617,402	
Owner-occupied housing units	36,587	48%	74,783,659	67%
Renter-occupied housing units	39,635	52%	36,833,743	33%
People age 25 and over with high school diploma or higher	125,881	96%	164,729,046	84%
People age 25 and over with bachelor's degree or higher	82,609	63%	52,948,622	27%
Foreign born	155,842	66%	37,547,789	13%
Number of people who speak a language other than English at home (population 5 years and older)	135,563	64%	55,807,878	20%
Median family income	$62,416		$58,526	
Per capita income	$22,155		$25,267	
Individuals living below the poverty level	30,879	13%	38,921,803	13%

Source: U.S. Bureau of the Census, 2006 American Community Survey estimates

GLOSSARY

abolition: The act of ending (abolishing) a particular practice or institution. It is most often used to describe the movement to end slavery.

abolitionist: Referring to a movement to end slavery. A person who opposes slavery and campaigns to end the practice.

aspiring: Hoping to get ahead in one's life or career.

assimilate: To adopt the customs and behaviors of a different group, culture, or country.

deported: Sent back to one's country of origin.

discriminate: To treat people differently or unfairly based on such factors as their race, nationality, ethnic group, or religion.

documentary: A film that presents factual information without any fictional story.

entrepreneurs: People who start their own businesses.

extremists: People whose political or religious beliefs go beyond what is generally accepted. Their extreme points of view may lead them to take drastic or violent action.

indentured servant: A person who is required to work for someone for a certain period of time, usually for a number of years.

plantain: A tropical fruit, similar to the banana, that is usually eaten cooked.

plantation: A large farm on which crops are grown to be sold.

polygamy: The practice of having more than one spouse.

prejudice: Negative judgments about a person or a group because of such things as race, religion, ethnic group, or economic status.

racism: Discrimination based on a person's or a group's race.

refugee: Someone who seeks or takes shelter in a foreign country, especially to avoid war, political persecution, or religious persecution in his or her native country.

supercomputers: The fastest, largest, and most powerful computers.

undocumented: Referring to immigrants who enter and remain in the United States without obtaining the permission and paperwork required by U.S. law.

Union: Another name for the United States, most commonly used before the twentieth century.

visa: A document that indicates a person has permission to enter the United States and to remain either permanently or for a certain period of time.

TO FIND OUT MORE

Further Reading

Blohm, Judith M., and Terri Lapinsky. *Kids Like Me: Voices of the Immigrant Experience*. Boston: Intercultural Press, 2006.

Brownell, Richard. *Immigration*. Farmington Hills, MI: Thomson Gale, 2008.

Levy, Patricia. *Nigeria*. New York: Marshall Cavendish Benchmark, 2004.

Olson, Kay Melchisedech. *Africans in America, 1619-1865*. Mankato, MN: Capstone Press, 2003.

Oppong, Joseph R. *Africa South of the Sahara*. New York: Chelsea House, 2005.

Websites

http://www.everyculture.com/Ge-It/Ghana.html
This section of the Multicultural America website offers an overview of the history and culture of Ghanaians in America.

http://www.everyculture.com/Ma-Ni/Nigeria.html
This section of the Multicultural America website offers an overview of the history and culture of Nigeria and Nigerians in America.

http://www.everyculture.com/multi/Le-Pa/Liberian-Americans.html
This section of the Multicultural America website offers an overview of the history and culture of Liberian Americans.

http://memory.loc.gov/learn/features/immig/african.html
This section of the Library of Congress website provides information about African immigration to the United States beginning with slavery and offers many links to primary sources.

BIBLIOGRAPHY

The author found these sources particularly helpful when researching this volume:

Chideya, Farai. "African Immigrants Confront American Dream." NPR, December 25, 2007. http://www.npr.org/templates/story/story.php?storyId = 17534100

Eissa, Salih Omar. "Diversity and Transformation: African Americans and African Immigration to the United States." American Immigration Law Foundation, March 2005. http://www.ailf.org

Meyers, Jessica. "African Refugees Reshape Dallas' Foreign Population." *Dallas Morning News*, June 24, 2008.

Roberts, Sam. "More Africans Enter U.S. Than in Days of Slavery." *New York Times*, February 21, 2005.

Takougang, Joseph. "Contemporary African Immigrants to the United States." *Ìrìnkèrindò: a Journal of African Migration*. http://www.africamigration.com/archive_02/j_takougang.htm

United Nations High Commissioner for Refugees. "Assistance to Refugees, Returnees, and Displaced Persons in Africa (Covering the Period 1 January 2007–15 June 2008." August 22, 2008, http://www.unhcr.org/excom/EXCOM/492d22c82.pdf

Notes:

Chapter 2:

Page 17: "Brethren, arise, arise . . ." "(1843) Henry Highland Garnet, 'An Address to the Slaves of the United States'," Blackpast.org, http://www.blackpast.org/?q = 1843-henry-highland-garnet-address-slaves-united-states

Chapter 3:

Page 34: "I can't understand why only in Africa . . ." *Pacific News Service*, June 5, 2003, http://news.pacificnews.org/news/view_article.html?article_id = 146bee055c4fe527fc2b4e9a32523438

Chapter 4:

Page 49: "The [immigrant] kids talk about . . ." November 15, 2005, http://frontpageafrica.com

Chapter 5:

Page 63: "It was overwhelming what needs to be done there . . ." Bentley, Brooke, "Okoye, NFL players return to Nigeria," HoustonTexans.com, May 16, 2008, http://www.houstontexans.com/community/Story.asp?story_id = 4325

All websites were accessible as of April 8, 2009.

INDEX

Page numbers in **boldface** are illustrations, tables, and charts.

About the Series Consultant

Judith Ann Warner is a Professor of Sociology and Criminal Justice at Texas A&M International University (TAMIU), located in Laredo, Texas, near the U.S.-Mexico border. She has specialized in the study of race and ethnic relations, focusing on new immigrants to the United States and their social incorporation into American society. Professor Warner is the editor of and contributed a number of essays to *Battleground Immigration* (2009), a collection of essays on immigration and related national security issues. Recognition of her work includes the 2007 Distance Educator of the Year Award and the 1991 Scholar of the Year Award at TAMIU.

About the Author

Jayne Keedle was born in England. She spent two years in Mexico City before immigrating to the United States at age sixteen. After graduating from the University of Connecticut with a degree in Latin American Studies, she worked as a newspaper journalist and then as an editor for *Weekly Reader* classroom magazines. She lives in Connecticut with husband, Jim, and stepdaughter, Alma. As a freelance writer and editor, she has written a number of books for young adults. Her books in the New Americans series are her first for Marshall Cavendish Benchmark.